To t...

WRINKLED
WISDOM

My great
re-discovered friend!

All the best
Bob Searles
"Soulie"

WRINKLED WISDOM

a collection of observations from
senior citizens throughout the ages

Compiled & edited
by Robert L. Searles, Jr.

TATE PUBLISHING & *Enterprises*

Published by Tate Publishing & Enterprises, LLC
127 E. Trade Center Terrace | Mustang, Oklahoma 73064 USA
1.888.361.9473 | www.tatepublishing.com

Tate Publishing is committed to excellence in the publishing industry. The company reflects the philosophy established by the founders, based on Psalm 68:11,
"The Lord gave the word and great was the company of those who published it."

Published in the United States of America

ISBN: 978-1-60799-594-4
Humor / Form / Anecdotes
10.02.08

"I am not young enough to know everything."

J. M. Barrie—Ernest, in The Admirable Crichton, Act 1.

TABLE OF CONTENTS

INTRODUCTION

One of the saddest realities of our youth–focused society is the popular belief that the elderly have little or nothing to contribute. Older parents and grandparents are frequently dismissed as rambling, out of touch with reality, or worse when they repeat stories or favorite sayings. It is not uncommon for younger family members to think they will never forget these stories because they have heard them too many times. It is also not uncommon for those same individuals to wish they could remember what the elders said after those voices are silenced.

In reality, much of the humor and wisdom of the world has come from "senior citizens" age fifty–five and older. Anyone who reaches this age can appreciate the brevity of life in a way that youth cannot. They have certainly experienced the pains of loss through death, sometimes untimely, among their own families and friends. They have also experienced some of the greatest joys life has to offer. Somehow, they all learned to survive, even thrive.

Things have certainly changed since the mid–twentieth century. Advances in transportation, communications, and technology have increased the pace of our world faster than anyone could have imagined fifty–five years ago. Medical advances and nutritional improvements give everyone the chance for an increasingly longer life. But human nature has not changed since Adam and Eve first walked in the garden of Eden.

The wisdom recorded in this book transcends the boundaries of time and place. Regardless of the obstacles these authors faced, the determination expressed in their words captures the unchanging truth about human nature. Their words have the power to spare us the agony of mistakes past and to give us the encouragement to embrace all the joys life has to offer.

During our year of researching, documenting, and recording quotations for this book, we made certain assumptions about the ages of the authors. Many quotes came from published manuscripts. For those, we list the author's age at publication date, realizing they were made some time prior to that date. For example, one of my favorite books by Duc de la Rochefoucauld François, *Sentences and Maximes Morales*, was published in 1678 when he was sixty–five years old. Therefore, all quotes from this book are attributed to François at age sixty–five. Other quotes come from writings, plays, books, and speeches. Some names are recognizable; others are not.

Regardless of their origin, this collection is a treasure trove of wit and wisdom that expresses the mastery of human observation. It is my hope that these pages will bring smiles, tears, and real insights about life to everyone who reads these gems of *Wrinkled Wisdom*.

THE AMERICAN EXPERIENCE

America is a country of young men.
Ralph Waldo Emerson, age 67 (1870)

Memory in America suffers amnesia.
Meridel Le Sueur, age 55 (1955)

We have forgotten that democracy must live as it
thinks and think as it lives.
Agnes Meyer, age 56 (1943)

In America everybody is of opinion that he has
no social superiors, since all men are equal, but
he does not admit that he has no social inferiors.
Bertrand Russell, age 78 (1950)

America is rather like life. You can usually
find in it what you look for ... It will probably
be interesting, and it is sure to be large.
E. M. Forster, age 68 (1951)

There is a need for heroism
in American life today.
Agnes Meyer, age 70 (1957)

What the United States does best is to understand
itself. What it does worst is understand others.
Carlos Fuentes, age 58 (1986)

I feel most at home in the United States, not
because it is intrinsically a more interesting country,
but because no one really belongs there any more
than I do. We are all there together in its
wholly excellent vacuum.
Wyndham Lewis, age 66 (1948)

The things that will destroy America are prosperity–
at–any–price, peace–at–any–price, safety–first
instead of duty–first, the love of soft living, and the
get–rich–quick theory of life.
Theodore Roosevelt, age 59 (1917)

It certainly must have been a relief for the women of the country to realize that one could be a woman and a lady and yet be thoroughly political.

Agnes Meyer, age 65 (1952)

America is a large, friendly dog in a very small room. Every time it wags its tail, it knocks over a chair.

A. J. Toynbee, age 65 (1954)

Woman's discontent increases in exact proportion to her development.

Elizabeth Cady Stanton, age 66 (1881)

Americans are very friendly and very suspicious, that is what Americans are and that is what always upsets the foreigner, who deals with them, they are so friendly how can they be so suspicious they are so suspicious how can they be so friendly but they just are.

Gertrude Stein, age 61 (1974)

The keynote of American civilization is a sort of warm-hearted vulgarity. The Americans have none of the irony of the English, none of their cool poise, none of their manner. But they do have friendliness. Where an Englishman would give you his card, an American would very likely give you his shirt.
Raymond Chandler, age 88 (1976)

In America nothing dies easier than tradition.
Russell Baker, age 66 (1991)

The [1950s]—they seem to have taken place on a sunny afternoon that asked nothing of you except a drifting belief in the moment and its power to satisfy.
Elizabeth Hardwick, age 67 (1983)

So—against odds, the women inch forward,
but I'm rather old to be carrying on this fight.
Eleanor Roosevelt, age 62 (1946)

The prolonged slavery of women is
the darkest page in human history.
Elizabeth Cady Stanton, age 66 (1881)

THE ARTS

At one time I thought he wanted to be an actor. He had certain qualifications, including no money and a total lack of responsibility.
Hedda Hopper, age 62 (1952)

Every young sculptor seems to think that he must give the world some specimen of indecorous womanhood, and call it Eve, Venus, a Nymph, or any name that may apologize for a lack of decent clothing.
Nathaniel Hawthorne, age 56 (1860)

[Rock 'n Roll is] the most brutal, ugly, desperate,
vicious form of expression it has been my
misfortune to hear.
Frank Sinatra, age 64 (1979)

Those who do not want to imitate
anything, produce nothing.
Salvador Dali, age 66 (1970)

For me, the cinema is not a slice of life,
but a piece of cake.
Alfred Hitchcock, age 78 (1977)

Drama is life with the dull bits cut out.
Alfred Hitchcock, age 85 (1984)

The artist doesn't have time to listen to
the critics. The ones who want to be writers
read the reviews, the ones who want to write
don't have the time to read reviews.
William Faulkner, age 61 (1958)

The only good copies are those which make
us see the absurdity of bad originals.
François, Duc De La Rochefoucauld, age 65 (1678)

I would rather be attacked than unnoticed. For the worst thing you can do to an author is to be silent as to his works. An assault upon a town is a bad thing; but starving it is still worse.

Samuel Johnson, age 70

Quoted in: James Boswell's
Life of Samuel Johnson, 26 March 1779 (1791)

If it's a good script I'll do it. And if it's a bad script, and they pay me enough, I'll do it.

George Burns, age 92 (1988)

BIRTH, LIFE, AND DEATH

For none shall die who have the future in them.
Meridel Le Sueur, age 55 (1955)

A happy childhood can't be cured. Mine'll
hang around my neck like a rainbow,
that's all, instead of a noose.
Hortense Calisher, age 60 (1971)

Although it is generally known, I think
it's about time to announce that I was
born at a very early age.
Groucho Marx, age 64 (1959)

Our birth is nothing but our death begun.
Edward Young, age 59

"Night Thoughts: The Complaint:
Night V" (1742–46)

What I call a good patient is one who, having
found a good physician, sticks to him till he dies.
Oliver Wendell Holmes, Sr., age 62 (1871)

Your body is the church where
Nature asks to be reverenced.
Marquis De Sade, age 57 (1797)

As for death one gets used to it, even if it's only
other people's death you get used to.
Enid Bagnold, age 80 (1969)

A belief in hell and the knowledge that every
ambition is doomed to frustration at the hands
of a skeleton have never prevented the majority
of human beings from behaving as though death
were no more than an unfounded rumor.
Aldous Huxley, age 56 (1950)

Because I could not stop for death,
He kindly stopped for me.
Emily Dickinson, age 61 (1891)

I will be conquered; I will not capitulate.
Samuel Johnson, age 73, on his deathbed. (1784)

There are all those early memories; one
cannot get another set; one has only those.
Willa Cather, age 58 (1931)

All men think all men mortal, but themselves.
Edward Young, age 59

"Night Thoughts: The Complaint:
Night 1" (1742–46)

BUSINESS

Executives are like joggers. If you stop a jogger, he goes on running on the spot. If you drag an executive away from his business, he goes on running on the spot, pawing the ground, talking business. He never stops hurtling onwards, making decisions and executing them.
Jean Baudrillard, age 58 (1990)

When you are skinning your customers you should leave some skin on to grow again so that you can skin them again.
Nikita Khrushchev, age 67 (1961)

People don't choose their careers;
they are engulfed by them.
John Dos Passos, age 64 (1959)

The reality is that zero defects in products plus zero
pollution plus zero risk on the job is equivalent
to maximum growth of government plus zero
economic growth plus runaway inflation.
Dixie Lee Ray, age 56 (1980)

CITIES AND CITY LIFE

We are in danger ... of making our cities
places where business goes on but where life,
in its real sense, is lost.
Hubert H. Humphrey, age 55 (1966)

A city is a place where there is no need to wait for
next week to get the answer to a question, to taste
the food of any country, to find new voices to
listen to and familiar ones to listen to again.
Margaret Mead, age 74 (1975)

Satan (impatiently) to Newcomer: The trouble with you Chicago people is, that you think you are the best people down here; whereas you are merely the most numerous.

Mark Twain, age 62 (1897)

There are three roads to ruin; women, gambling and technicians. The most pleasant is with women, the quickest is with gambling, but the surest is with technicians.

Georges Pompidou, age 57

Quoted in: *Sunday Telegraph*
(London, 26 May 1968)

I had very good dentures once. Some magnificent gold work. It's the only form of jewelry a man can wear that women fully appreciate.

Graham Greene, age 65

Mr. Visconti in *Travels with My Aunt*, part 2, chapter 7 (1969)

EDUCATION

One is not born a genius, one becomes a genius.
Simone de Beauvoir, age 65 (1973)

The liberally educated person is one who is able
to resist the easy and preferred answers, not
because he is obstinate but because he knows
others worthy of consideration.
Allan Bloom, age 57 (1987)

People commonly educate their children as they
build their houses, according to some plan they
think beautiful, without considering whether it is
suited to the purposes for which they are designed.
Lady Mary Wortley Montagu, age 61 (1970)

Education costs money, but then so does ignorance.
Sir Claus Moser, age 68 (1990)

A change of heart is the essence of all
other change and it is brought about
by re–education of the mind.
Emmeline Pethick–Lawrence, age 71 (1938)

A teacher affects eternity; he can never
tell where his influence stops.
Henry B. Adams, age 69 (1907)

One of the benefits of a college education
is to show the boy its little avail.
Ralph Waldo Emerson, age 67 (1870)

And yet, in the schoolroom more than any
other place, does the difference of sex, if
there is any, need to be forgotten.
Susan B. Anthony, age 55 (1873)

The medieval university looked backwards;
it professed to be a storehouse of old
knowledge ... The modern university looks
forward, and is a factory of new knowledge.
Thomas Henry Huxley, age 67 (1892)

University degrees are a bit like adultery: you may
not want to get involved with that sort of thing,
but you don't want to be thought incapable.
Sir Peter Imbert, age 59 (1992)

A single fact lies at the source of all
deviations, viz., that the child has been
prevented from fulfilling the original pattern
of his development at the formative age...
Maria Montessori, age 69 (1939)

Life is amazing: and the teacher had better prepare
himself to be a medium for that amazement.
Edward Blishen, age 63 (1983)

Housework is a breeze. Cooking is a pleasant
diversion. Putting up a retaining wall is a lark. But
teaching is like climbing a mountain.
Fawn M. Brodie, age 62 (1977)

We teachers can only help the work going on,

as servants wait upon a master.

Maria Montessori, age 79 (1949)

EMOTIONS

We are so vain that we even care for
the opinion of those we don't care for.
Marie Ebner von Eschenbach, age 75 (1905)

My mother used to say, "He who angers you,
conquers you!" But my mother was a saint.
Elizabeth Kenny, age 57 (1943)

Hate traps us by binding us too
tightly to our adversary.
Milan Kundera, age 62 (1991)

He has not learned the lesson of life who
does not every day surmount a fear.
Ralph Waldo Emerson, age 67 (1870)

He who believes in freedom of the will
has never loved and never hated.
Marie Ebner von Eschenbach, age 75 (1905)

There is only one passion, the passion for happiness.
Denis Diderot, age 61 (1966)

Humour brings insight and tolerance. Irony
brings a deeper and less friendly understanding.
Agnes Repplier, age 78 (1936)

Jealousy, that dragon which slays love
under the pretence of keeping it alive.
Havelock Ellis, age 78 (1937)

People need joy quite as much as clothing.
Some of them need it far more.
Margaret Collier Graham, age 56 (1906)

The passions are the only orators
which always persuade.
François, Duc De La Rochefoucauld, age 65 (1678)

It is quite gratifying to feel guilty if you haven't
done anything wrong: how noble! Whereas it
is rather hard and certainly depressing to
admit guilt and to repent.
Hannah Arendt, age 57 (1963)

Happiness makes up in height what it lacks in length.
Robert Frost, age 68 (1942)

To make oneself hated is more difficult
than to make oneself loved.
Pablo Picasso, age 75 (1956)

I never like being hit without striking back.
Joseph Chamberlain, age 67 (1903)

Always remember, others may hate you.
Those who hate you don't win unless you
hate them. And then you destroy yourself.
Richard M. Nixon, age 61 (1974)

Conquer, but don't triumph.
Marie Ebner von Eschenbach, age 75 (1905)

When we think of cruelty, we must try to
remember the stupidity, the envy, the
frustration from which it has arisen.
Edith Sitwell, age 78 (1965)

We are truly indefatigable in providing for
the needs of the body, but we starve the soul.
Ellen Wood, age 73 (1883)

My vigor, vitality and cheek repel me. I
am the kind of woman I would run from.
Nancy Astor, age 76 (1955)

FRIENDS AND FRIENDSHIP

The richer your friends, the more they will cost you.
Elisabeth Marbury, age 67 (1923)

It is not fair to ask of others what
you are willing to do yourself.
Eleanor Roosevelt, age 62 (1946)

Treat your friends as you do your pictures,
and place them in their best light.
Jennie Jerome Churchill, age 62 (1916)

I can't forgive my friends for dying; I don't find
these vanishing acts of theirs at all amusing.
Logan Pearsall Smith, age 66 (1931)

I do not believe that friends are necessarily
the people you like best, they are merely
the people who got there first.
Peter Ustinov, age 56 (1977)

It is easy enough to be friendly to one's friends.
But to befriend the one who regards himself as
your enemy is the quintessence of true religion.
The other is mere business.
Mohandas K. Gandhi, age 79 (1948)

If you think it's hard to meet new people,
try picking up the wrong golf ball.
Jack Lemmon, age 60 (1985)

When women kiss it always reminds
one of prize–fighters shaking hands.
H. L. Mencken, age 69 (1949)

Friend, what years could us divide?
Dinah Mulock Craik, age 55 (1881)

HUMAN NATURE

Promises that you make to yourself are often like
the Japanese plum tree—they bear no fruit.
Frances Marion, age 62 (1972)

People who fight fire with fire
usually end up with ashes.
Abigail Van Buren, age 56 (1974)

Without discipline, there's no life at all.
Katherine Hepburn, age 66 (1975)

Whenever two good people argue
over principles, they are both right.
Marie Ebner von Eschenbach, age 75 (1905)

Always do right—this will gratify
some and astonish the rest.
Mark Twain, age 66 (1901)

Would that well–thinking people should
be replaced by thinking ones.
Natalie Clifford Barney, age 86 (1962)

We have to face the fact that either all
of us are going to die together or we are
going to learn to live together and if we are
to live together we have to talk.
Eleanor Roosevelt, age 76 (1960)

Nothing so needs reforming
as other people's habits.
Mark Twain, age 59 (1894)

Moderation is a virtue only in those
who are thought to have an alternative.
Henry Kissinger, age 59 (1982)

As far as your self–control goes,
as far goes your freedom.
Marie Ebner von Eschenbach, age 75 (1905)

Character builds slowly, but it can be
torn down with incredible swiftness.
Faith Baldwin, age 69 (1962)

Memory is more indelible than ink.
Anita Loos, age 85 (1974)

Perfection is a trifle dull. It is not the
least of life's ironies that this, which we all
aim at, is better not quite achieved.
W. Somerset Maugham, age 64 (1938)

One is forever throwing away
substance for shadows.
Jennie Jerome Churchill, age 60 (1914)

There is no sadder sight than a young
pessimist, except an old optimist.
Mark Twain, age 68 (1903)

The skeptic does not mean him who doubts, but him who investigates or researches, as opposed to him who asserts and thinks that he has found.
Miguel De Unamuno, age 60 (1924)

"All that's in the past. All that's over and done with."
"Of course, Tonton, until it begins again."
Colette, age 71 (1944)

If you do not tell the truth about yourself you cannot tell it about other people.
Virginia Woolf, age 70 (1941)

If one does not understand a person,
one tends to regard him as a fool.
Carl Jung, age 80 (1955)

Don't be too nice to me. When anyone's
too nice to me, I don't know what I'm doing—
I boil over like a soup.
Colette, age 71 (1944)

As if one could know the good a person is capable
of, when one doesn't know the bad he might do.
Elias Canetti, age 68 (1991)

We seldom find people ungrateful so long as we
are in a condition to render them service.
François, Duc De La Rochefoucauld, age 65 (1678)

People who bite the hand that feeds them
usually lick the boot that kicks them.
Eric Hoffer, age 71 (1973)

The height of cleverness is being able to conceal it.
François, Duc De La Rochefoucauld, age 65 (1678)

There are no good girls gone wrong,
just bad girls found out.
Mae West, age 82 (1975)

So much of our lives is given over to the
consideration of our imperfections that
there is no time to improve our imaginary
virtues. The truth is we only perfect our vices,
and man is a worse creature when he dies than
he was when he was born.
Edward Dahlberg, age 64 (1964)

The weak have one weapon: the errors
of those who think they are strong.
Georges Bidault, age 63 (1962)

Most virtue is a demand for greater seduction.
Natalie Clifford Barney, age 88 (1962)

Man seems to be capable of great virtues
but not of small virtues; capable of defying
his torturer but not of keeping his temper.

G. K. Chesterton, age 62 (1936)

Nature has not got two voices, you know,
one of them condemning all day what
the other commands.

Marquis De Sade, age 55 (1795)

Possibly, more people kill themselves and
others out of hurt vanity than out of envy,
jealousy, malice or desire for revenge.

Iris Murdoch, age 64 (1983)

There are no grades of vanity, there are
only grades of ability in concealing it.
Mark Twain, age 63 (1898)

Scratching is one of nature's sweetest
gratifications, and the one nearest at hand.
Michel De Montaigne, age 55 (1588)

Sometimes a neighbor whom we have disliked a
lifetime for his arrogance and conceit lets fall a
single commonplace remark that shows us another
side, another man, really; a man uncertain, and
puzzled, and in the dark like ourselves.
Willa Cather, age 58 (1931)

The truth is that we live out our lives putting off all that can be put off; perhaps we all know deep down that we are immortal and that sooner or later all men will do and know all things.

Jorge Luis Borges, age 65 (1964)

Procrastination is the thief of time.

Edward Young, age 59

"Night Thoughts: The Complaint: Night 1" (1742–46)

There are incalculable resources in the human spirit, once it has been set free.

Hubert H. Humphrey, age 55 (1966)

Gossip is news running ahead
of itself in a red satin dress.
Liz Smith, age 62 (1985)

Of course I lie to people. But I lie altruistically—for
our mutual good. The lie is the basic building block
of good manners. That may seem mildly shocking
to a moralist—but then what isn't?
Quentin Crisp, age 76 (1984)

Sir [to a boring guest], you have but two topics,
yourself and me. I am sick of both.
Samuel Johnson, age 67

Quoted in: James Boswell, *Life of Samuel Johnson*,
May 1776 (1791)

There couldn't be a society of people who didn't dream. They'd be dead in two weeks.
William Burroughs, age 60 (1981)

Dreams come true; without that possibility, nature would not incite us to have them.
John Updike, age 67 (1989)

To be able to fill leisure intelligently is the last product of civilization.
Bertrand Russell, age 58 (1930)

If I cannot brag of knowing something, then
I brag of not knowing it; at any rate, brag.
Ralph Waldo Emerson, age 63 (1866)

Only man is not content to leave things as they are
but must always be changing them, and when he
has done so, is seldom satisfied with the result.
Elspeth Huxley, age 55 (1962)

He who lives without folly isn't so wise as he thinks.
François, Duc De La Rochefoucauld, age 65 (1678)

Imaginary pains are by far the most real
we suffer, since we feel a constant need for
them and invent them because there is no
way of doing without them.
E. M. Cioran, age 62 (1973)

Depend upon it that if a man talks of his
misfortunes there is something in them
that is not disagreeable to him.
Samuel Johnson, age 71

Quoted in: James Boswell's *Life of Samuel Johnson*,
1780 entry (1791)

A man's conscience and his judgement [are] the same thing; and as the judgement, so also the conscience, may be erroneous.
Thomas Hobbes, age 63 (1651)

If we had no faults of our own, we should not take so much pleasure in noticing those in others.
François, Duc De La Rochefoucauld, age 65 (1678)

A lie will easily get you out of a scrape, and yet, strangely and beautifully, rapture possesses you when you have taken the scrape and left out the lie.
C. E. Montague, age 55 (1922)

It is said that desire is a product of the will, but the converse is in fact true: will is a product of desire.

Denis Diderot, age 61

Elements of Physiology, "Will, Freedom" (notes written 1774–80; first published 1875; repr. in Selected Writings, ed. by Lester G. Crocker, 1966)

Eccentricity is not, as dull people would
have us believe, a form of madness. It is
often a kind of innocent pride, and the man
of genius and the aristocrat are frequently
regarded as eccentrics because genius and
aristocrat are entirely unafraid of and
uninfluenced by the opinions and
vagaries of the crowd.
Edith Sitwell, age 78 (1965)

Man is the only animal that blushes. Or needs to.
Mark Twain, age 62 (1897)

If you pick up a starving dog and make him prosperous, he will not bite you. This is the principal difference between a dog and a man.
Mark Twain, age 59 (1894)

Mistakes are, after all, the foundations of truth, and if a man does not know what a thing is, it is at least an increase in knowledge if he knows what it is not.
Carl Jung, age 84 (1951)

The young man who has not wept is a savage, and the old man who will not laugh is a fool.
George Santayana, age 62 (1925)

Few things are harder to put up with
than the annoyance of a good example.
Mark Twain, age 59 (1894)

Our greatest foes, and whom we
must chiefly combat, are within.
Miguel De Cervantes, age 68 (1615)

Both men and women are fallible.
The difference is, women know it.
Eleanor Bron, age 58 (1992)

A life spent in making mistakes is not
only more honorable but more useful than
a life spent doing nothing.
George Bernard Shaw, age 55 (1911)

Excess on occasion is exhilarating.
It prevents moderation from acquiring
the deadening effect of habit.
W. Somerset Maugham, age 64 (1938)

Nothing sets a person up more than having
something turn out just the way it's supposed to be,
like falling into a Swiss snowdrift and seeing a big dog
come up with a little cask of brandy round its neck.
Claud Cockburn, age 77 (1981)

A fairly bright boy is far more intelligent and far
better company than the average adult.
J. B. S. Haldane, age 56 (1948)

Among those whom I like or admire, I can find no
common denominator, but among those whom I
love, I can: all of them make me laugh.
W. H. Auden, age 55 (1962)

You must have been warned against letting the
golden hours slip by. Yes, but some of them are
golden only because we let them slip.
J. M. Barrie, age 62 (1922)

LIVING AND AGING

In youth, we learn; in age, we understand.
Marie Ebner von Eschenbach, age 75 (1905)

Being seventy is not a sin.
Golda Meir, age 73 (1971)

Since it is the Other within us who is old,
it is natural that the revelation of our age
should come to us from outside—from others.
We do not accept it willingly.
Simone de Beauvoir, age 64 (1972)

When you're old, everything
you do is sort of a miracle.
Millicent Fenwick, age 71 (1981)

I enjoy my wrinkles and regard them as badges of
distinction—I've worked hard for them!
Maggie Kuhn, age 74 (1979)

Twenty can't be expected to tolerate sixty
in all things, and sixty gets bored stiff with
twenty's eternal love affairs.
Emily Carr, age 63

Hundreds and Thousands: The Journals of Emily Carr
(1966), entry for 12 Aug. 1934

Young men are apt to think themselves wise
enough, as drunken men are apt to think
themselves sober enough.
Lord Chesterfield, age 59 (1753)

The young always have the same problem—
how to rebel and conform at the same time.
They have now solved this by defying their
parents and copying one another.
Quentin Crisp, age 60 (1968)

Old age is the verdict of life.
Amelia Barr, age 82 (1913)

If youth but knew; if age but could.
Henri Estienne, age 63 (1594)

I instinctively like to acquire and store
up what promises to outlast me.
Colette, age 55 (1928)

Youth doesn't reason, it acts. The old man reasons
and would like to make the others act in his place.
Francis Picabia, age 74 (1952)

The trouble with most women is they get old in
their heads. They think about it too much.
Josephine Baker, age 64 (1970)

I have so much to do every morning that I don't
have any time to think about getting old.
Claude D. Pepper, age 88 (1988)

Old age is not a disease—it is strength and
survivorship, triumph over all kinds of vicissitudes
and disappointments, trials and illnesses.
Maggie Kuhn, age 74 (1979)

Everyone complains of his memory,
none of his judgment.
François, Duc De La Rochefoucauld, age 65 (1678)

How old would you be if you
didn't know how old you are?
Satchel Paige, age 74 (1978)

Life is an end in itself, and the only question
as to whether it is worth living is whether
you have had enough of it.
Oliver Wendell Holmes, Jr., age 59 (1900)

I am not half as patient with old
women now that I am one.
Emily Carr, age 69 (1940)

Live all you can; it's a mistake not to.
It doesn't so much matter what you do in
particular, so long as you have your life.
If you haven't had that what have you had?
Henry James, age 60 (1903)

By the time we hit fifty, we have learned our hardest
lessons. We have found out that only a few things
are really important. We have learned to take life
seriously, but never ourselves.
Marie Dressler, age 61 (1934)

The years between fifty and seventy are the hardest.
You are always being asked to do things, and yet
you are not decrepit enough to turn them down.
T. S. Eliot, age 62 (1950)

I wish I had started out at the age of ninety–six,
look how much fun I would have had.
Eubie Blake, age 96 (1979)

There is no cure for birth and death
save to enjoy the interval.
George Santayana, age 59 (1922)

Our technological society scrap–piles
old people as it does automobiles
Maggie Kuhn, (1979)

The fact that life has no meaning is a reason
to live—moreover, the only one.
E. M. Cioran, age 75 (1986)

I don't feel old, just downright worn out.
Will Smith, age 110 (1987)

Every age is reminded by what it hears, that what has been done can be done again. Transgressions never die from the passage of age; crime is never erased by time; vice is never buried in oblivion.

Saint Cyrian, age 56 (246 AD)

If a man can reach the latter days of his life with his soul intact, he has mastered life.

Gordon Parks, age 77 (1989)

Old age is the verdict of life.

Amelia Barr, age 82 (1913)

When I was forty and looking at sixty, it seemed
like a thousand years away. But sixty–two feels
like a week and a half away from eighty.
I must now get on with those things I always
talked about doing but put off.
Harry Belafonte, age 62 (1989)

To me, old age is always fifteen
years older than I am.
Bernard Baruch, age 85 (1955)

Lord Tyrawley and I have been dead these two years, but we don't choose to have it known.
Lord Chesterfield, age 79

Quoted in: James Boswell's *Life of Samuel Johnson*, 3 April 1773 (1791)

I have a lifetime appointment and I intend to serve it. I expect to die at 110, shot by a jealous husband.
Justice Thurgood Marshall, age 82 (1990)

I advise you to go on living solely to enrage those who are paying your annuities. It is the only pleasure I have left.
Voltaire, age 60 (1754)

I hope I never get so old I get religious.
Ingmar Bergman, age 71 (1989)

I have been asked how I grow old so easily.
The answer is: I give all my time to it.
Emanuel Celler, age 88 (1971)

Old age isn't so bad when you
consider the alternative.
Maurice Chevalier, age 72 (1960)

Old age, believe me, is a good and pleasant thing.
It is true you are gently shouldered off the stage,
but then you are given such a comfortable
front stall as spectator.
Jane Harrison, age 75 (1925)

Old people love to give good advice to
console themselves for no longer being able
to set a bad example.
François, Duc De La Rochefoucauld, age 65 (1678)

Age is not a particularly interesting subject. Anyone
can get old. All you have to do is live long enough.
Groucho Marx, age 64 (1959)

For each of us, after middle–age,
the world is always emptying.
Daisy, Princess of Pless, age 63 (1931)

If you associate enough with older people who do
enjoy their lives, who are not stored away in any
golden ghettos, you will gain a sense of continuity
and of the possibility for a full life.
Margaret Mead, age 76 (1977)

If you are idle, be not solitary;
if you are solitary, be not idle.
Samuel Johnson, age 70

Letter, 27 Oct. 1779, to James Boswell. Quoted in:
James Boswell's *Life of Samuel Johnson* (1791)

When you get to my age life seems little more
than one long march to and from the lavatory.
John Mortimer, age 65 (1988)

Growing old is no more than a bad habit
which a busy man has no time to form.
Andre Maurois, age 65 (1940)

We need not only a purpose in life to give meaning to our existence but also something to give meaning to our suffering. We need as much something to suffer for as something to live for.

Eric Hoffer, age 71 (1973)

LOVE AND MARRIAGE

The fate of love is that it always
seems too little or too much.
Amelia Barr, age 72 (1904)

Love is moral even without legal marriage,
but marriage is immoral without love.
Ellen Key, age 63 (1911)

In real love you want the other person's good.
In romantic love you want the other person.
Margaret Anderson, age 76 (1969)

In our monogamous part of the world, to marry
means to halve one's rights and double one's duties.
Arthur Schopenhauer, age 63 (1851)

Great loves too must be endured.
Coco Chanel, age 88 (1971)

Husbands never become good;
they merely become proficient.
H. L. Mencken, age 69 (1949)

It is disaster to have a man fall in love with me.
They aren't content to take what I can give,
they want everything from me.
Katherine Anne Porter, age 84 (1974)

True love is like ghosts, which everyone
talks about but few have seen.
François, Duc De La Rochefoucauld, age 65 (1678)

The formula for achieving a successful relationship
is simple: you should treat all disasters as if
they were trivialities but never treat a triviality
as if it were a disaster.
Quentin Crisp, age 72 (1984)

Wedlock's a lane where there is no turning.
Dinah Mulock Craik, age 55 (1881)

Women have changed in their relationship to men,
but men stand pat just where Adam did when it
comes to dealing with women.
Dorothy Dix, age 65 (1926)

I come to fetch my heart where I left it,
that is to say in yours.
Juliette Drouet, age 75 (1881)

The majority of persons choose their wives with as little prudence as they eat. They see a trull with nothing else to recommend her but a pair of thighs and choice hunkers, and so smart to void their seed that they marry her at once. They imagine they can live in marvelous contentment with handsome feet and ambrosial buttocks. Most men are accredited fools shortly after they leave the womb.

Edward Dahlberg, age 68 (1968)

A man would prefer to come home to an unmade bed and a happy woman than to a neatly made bed and an angry woman.

Marlene Dietrich, age 58 (1962)

A woman despises a man for loving her,
unless she returns his love.
Elizabeth Stoddard, age 65 (1888)

If you want to know about a man, you can find
out an awful lot by looking at who he married.
Kirk Douglas, age 72 (1988)

So many persons think divorce a panacea for
every ill, who find out, when they try it, that
the remedy is worse than the disease.
Dorothy Dix, age 65 (1926)

An ideal wife is any woman
who has an ideal husband.
Booth Tarkington, age 57 (1926)

Divorce is probably of nearly the same date as
marriage. I believe, however, that marriage is
some weeks the more ancient.
Voltaire, age 70 (1764)

The reason that husbands and wives do
not understand each other is because
they belong to different sexes.
Dorothy Dix, age 65 (1926)

MEN AND WOMEN

Women like to sit down with
trouble as if it were knitting.
Ellen Glasgow, age 58 (1932)

It will all go on as long as women are stupid
enough to go on bringing men into the world...
Dorothy Miller Richardson, age 65 (1938)

Women can't have an honest exchange in front
of men without having it called a cat fight.
Clare Boothe Luce, age 72 (1975)

Plain women know more about
men than beautiful ones do.
Katherine Hepburn, age 66 (1975)

Men greet each other with a sock on the arm,
women with a hug, and the hug wears
better in the long run.
Edward Hoagland, age 56 (1988)

Male supremacy has kept woman down.
It has not knocked her out.
Clare Boothe Luce, age 71 (1974)

Men have a much better time of it than women.
For one thing, they marry later, for another thing,
they die earlier.
H. L. Mencken, age 69 (1949)

A man's home may seem to be his castle on the
outside; inside, it is more often his nursery.
Clare Boothe Luce, age 71 (1974)

You have to be very fond of men. Very, very fond.
You have to be very fond of them to love them.
Otherwise they're simply unbearable.
Marguerite Duras, age 73 (1990)

Whatever women do they must do twice
as well as men to be thought half as good.
Luckily, this is not difficult.
Charlotte Whitton, age 67 (1963)

It is much more easy to accuse the
one sex than to excuse the other.
Michel De Montaigne, age 55 (1588)

Too often the great decisions are originated
and given form in bodies made up wholly of men,
or so completely dominated by them that
whatever of special value women have to
offer is shunted aside without expression.
Eleanor Roosevelt, age 68 (1952)

Bachelors know more about women than married
men. If they didn't they'd be married, too.
H. L. Mencken, age 69 (1949)

Men who are unhappy, like men who sleep badly,
are always proud of the fact.
Bertrand Russell, age 58 (1930)

We have dreamt of every woman there is, and
dreamt too of the miracle that would bring us the
pleasure of being a woman, for women have all the
qualities—courage, passion, the capacity to love,
cunning—whereas all our imagination can do is
naively pile up the illusion of courage.
Jean Baudrillard, age 58 (1987)

Women are a sisterhood. They make common
cause in behalf of the sex; and, indeed, this is
natural enough, when we consider the vast
power that the law gives us over them.
William Cobbett, age 67 (1829)

The queens in history compare
favorably with the kings.
Elizabeth Cady Stanton, age 66 (1881)

When a woman behaves like a man, why
doesn't she behave like a nice man?
Dame Edith Evans, age 68 (1956)

But if God had wanted us to think just with
our wombs, why did He give us a brain?
Clare Boothe Luce, age 67 (1970)

A woman is like a teabag—only in hot
water do you realize how strong she is.
Nancy Reagan, age 58 (1981)

Most women defend themselves. It is the female of
the species—it is the tigress and lioness in you—
which tends to defend when attacked.
Margaret Thatcher, age 64 (1989)

If there hadn't been women, we'd still be squatting in a cave eating raw meat, because we made civilization in order to impress our girl friends. And they tolerated it and let us go ahead and play with our toys.
Orson Welles, age 55 (1970)

It seems as though women keep growing. Eventually they can have little or nothing in common with the men they chose long ago.
Eugenie Clark, age 57 (1979)

The cocks may crow,
but it's the hen that lays the egg.
Margaret Thatcher, age 64 (1989)

For despite their achievements, the world has not
been willing to accept the contributions
that women have made.
Mary McLeod Bethune, age 60 (1935)

MISCELLANEOUS

Modern inventions have banished the
spinning wheel, and the same law of progress
makes the woman of today a different woman
from her grandmother.
Elizabeth Cady Stanton, age 66 (1881)

Compromise makes a good
umbrella but a poor roof.
James Russell Lowell, age 67 (1884)

A fanatic is one who can't change his
mind and won't change the subject.
Sir Winston Churchill, age 80 (1954)

Sincerity: if you can fake it, you've got it made.
Daniel Schorr, age 58 (1992)

Mere human beings can't afford to be fanatical
about anything...Not even about justice or loyalty.
The fanatic for justice ends by murdering a
million helpless people to clear a space for
his law–courts. If we are to survive on
this planet, there must be compromises.
Storm Jameson, age 66 (1957)

Put all your eggs in the one basket and—
watch that basket.
Mark Twain, age 59 (1894)

Information can tell us everything. It has all the answers. But they are answers to questions we have not asked, and which doubtless don't even arise.
Jean Baudrillard, age 58 (1987)

Because people have no thoughts to deal in, they deal cards, and try and win one another's money. Idiots!
Arthur Schopenhauer, age 63 (1851)

My favorite animal is the mule. He has a lot more horse sense than a horse. He knows when to stop eating. And he knows when to stop working.
Harry S. Truman, age 68 (1952)

Declaration of Sentiment... We hold these
truths to be self–evident: that all men
and women are created equal...
Elizabeth Cady Stanton, age 66 (1881)

I feel no flattery when people speak of my voice. I'm
simply grateful that I found a way to work around
my impairment. Once a stutterer, always a stutterer.
If I get any credit for the way I sound, I accept it in
the name of those of us who are impaired.
James Earl Jones, age 59 (1990)

It is useless for the sheep to pass resolutions in
favour of vegetarianism, while the
wolf remains of a different opinion.
W. R. Inge, age 55 (1915)

All my life through, the new sights of
Nature made me rejoice like a child.
Marie Curie, age 56 (1923)

Perhaps there is only one cardinal sin: impatience.
Because of impatience we were driven out of
Paradise, because of impatience we cannot return.
W. H. Auden, age 55 (1962)

If there were only one truth, you couldn't
paint a hundred canvases on the same theme.
Pablo Picasso, age 85

Quoted in: Hélène Parmelin, *Picasso Says...* "Truth"
(1966; tr. 1969)

Truth is the most valuable thing we have.
Let us economize it.
Mark Twain, age 62 (1897)

Not only will atomic power be released, but someday we will harness the rise and fall of the tides and imprison the rays of the sun.
Thomas Alva Edison, age 74 (1921)

Everything holds its breath except spring. She bursts through as strong as ever.
Emily Carr, age 69 (1940)

Familiarity breeds contempt. How accurate that is. The reason we hold truth in such respect is because we have so little opportunity to get familiar with it.
Mark Twain, age 63 (1898)

In this world nothing can be said to
be certain, except death and taxes.
Benjamin Franklin, age 83 (1789)

God gave us memory so that we
might have roses in December.
J. M. Barrie, age 62 (1922)

It rarely adds anything to say, "In my opinion"—
not even modesty. Naturally a sentence is only
your opinion; and you are not the Pope.
Paul Goodman, age 55 (1966)

I am extraordinarily patient provided
I get my own way in the end.
Margaret Thatcher, age 58 (1983)

I was proud of the youths who opposed the
war in Vietnam because they were my babies.
Benjamin Spock, age 85 (1988)

History is the present. That's why every generation
writes it anew. But what most people think of
as history is its end product, myth.
E. L. Doctorow, age 57 (1988)

As there is a use in medicine for poisons,
so the world cannot move without rogues.
Ralph Waldo Emerson, age 57 (1860)

Man, as long as he lives, is immortal.
One minute before his death he shall be immortal.
But one minute later, God wins.
Elie Wiesel, age 60

Interview in Writers at Work (Eighth Series, ed. George
Plimpton, 1988), paraphrasing Jewish tradition.

Smokers, male and female, inject and
excuse idleness in their lives every time
they light a cigarette.
Colette, age 60 (1933)

A decent provision for the poor
is the true test of civilization.
Samuel Johnson, age 61

Quoted by the Rev. Dr. Maxwell in: James Boswell's
Life of Samuel Johnson (1791), 1770 entry.

The past is a foreign country;
they do things differently there.
L. P. Hartley, age 58 (1953)

What a delightful thing is the conversation
of specialists! One understands absolutely
nothing and it's charming.
Edgar Degas, age 58 (1892, in *Degas Letters*,
Appendix; ed. by Marcel Guerin, 1947)

Flattery corrupts both the receiver and the giver.
Edmund Burke, age 61 (1790)

I hate flowers—I paint them because they're
cheaper than models and they don't move.
Georgia O'Keeffe, age 67 (1954)

The future? Like unwritten books and
unborn children, you don't talk about it.
Dietrich Fischer–Dieskau, age 63 (1988)

The first day a man is a guest,
the second a burden, the third a pest.
Edouard Laboulaye, age 60 (1871)

The feeling of being hurried is not usually the result
of living a full life and having no time. It is on the
contrary born of a vague fear that we are wasting
our life. When we do not do the one thing we
ought to do, we have no time for anything else—
we are the busiest people in the world.
Eric Hoffer, age 70 (1973)

If I were asked to name the chief benefit of the house, I should say: the house shelters day–dreaming, the house protects the dreamer, the house allows one to dream in peace.

Gaston Bachelard, age 72 (1958)

An empty head is not really empty; it is stuffed with rubbish. Hence the difficulty of forcing anything into an empty head.

Eric Hoffer, age 71 (1973)

Bias and impartiality is in the eye of the beholder.

Lord Barnett, age 67 (1990)

You mustn't always believe what I say.
Questions tempt you to tell lies,
particularly when there is no answer.
Pablo Picasso, age 77 (1958)

I remain just one thing, and one thing only—
and that is a clown. It places me on a far
higher plane than any politician.
Charlie Chaplin, age 71 (1960)

I have tried too in my time to be a philosopher;
but, I don't know how, cheerfulness
was always breaking in.
Oliver Edwards, age 67 (1778)

In philosophy, if you aren't moving at
a snail's pace, you aren't moving at all.
Iris Murdoch, age 68 (1986)

MONEY AND FINANCE

Money is a poor man's credit card.

Marshall McLuhan, age 60 (1971)

Between persons of equal income there is no social distinction except the distinction of merit. Money is nothing: character, conduct, and capacity are everything... There would be great people and ordinary people and little people, but the great would always be those who had done great things, and never the idiots whose mothers had spoiled them and whose fathers had left them a hundred thousand a year; and the little would be persons of small minds and mean characters, and not poor persons who had never had a chance. That is why idiots are always in favour of inequality of income (their only chance of eminence), and the really great in favour of equality.

George Bernard Shaw, age 72 (1928)

When it comes to finances, remember that there
are no withholding taxes on the wages of sin.
Mae West, age 82 (1975)

What is called generosity is usually only the
vanity of giving; we enjoy the vanity more
than the thing given.
François, Duc De La Rochefoucauld, age 65 (1678)

No one would remember the Good Samaritan
if he'd only had good intentions—
he had money as well.
Margaret Thatcher, age 61 (1986)

There is no finer investment for any
community than putting milk into babies.
Sir Winston Churchill, age 69 (1974)

Prosperity is only an instrument to be used,
not a deity to be worshiped.
Calvin Coolidge, age 56 (1928)

There is a gigantic difference between earning
a great deal of money and being rich.
Marlene Dietrich, age 61 (1962)

Wealth is in applications of mind to nature; and
the art of getting rich consists not in industry,
much less in saving, but in a better order,
in timeliness, in being at the right spot.
Ralph Waldo Emerson, age 57 (1860)

Wealth, in even the most improbable cases,
manages to convey the aspect of intelligence.
John Kenneth Galbraith, age 74 (1982)

If you can actually count your money,
then you are not really a rich man.
J. Paul Getty, age 65 (1957)

There must be a reason why some people can afford to live well. They must have worked for it. I only feel angry when I see waste. When I see people throwing away things that we could use.
Mother Teresa, age 65 (1975)

October. This is one of the peculiarly dangerous months to speculate in stocks in. The others are July, January, September, April, November, May, March, June, December, August, and February.
Mark Twain, age 59 (1894)

Man hoards himself when he has nothing to give away.
Edward Dahlberg, age 65 (1965)

It is wonderful to think how men of very large estates not only spend their yearly income, but are often actually in want of money. It is clear, they have not value for what they spend.

Samuel Johnson, age 69

Quoted in: James Boswell's *Life of Samuel Johnson*, 10 April 1778 (1791)

The wretchedness of being rich is that you live with rich people...To suppose, as we all suppose, that we could be rich and not behave as the rich behave, is like supposing that we could drink all day and stay sober.

Logan Pearsall Smith, age 66 (1931)

There are two times in a man's life when
he should not speculate: when he can't afford it,
and when he can.
Mark Twain, age 62 (1897)

PARENTS AND FAMILIES

Being a mother is a noble status, right? Right.
So why does it change when you put "unwed"
or "welfare" in front of it?
Florynce R. Kennedy, Esq., age 57 (1973)

Fathers and mothers have lost the idea that
the highest aspiration they might have for
their children is for them to be wise…
specialized competence and success are all
that they can imagine.
Allan Bloom, age 57 (1987)

What the Nation must realize is that the home,
when both parents work, is non–existent.
Once we have honestly faced that fact,
we must act accordingly.
Agnes Meyer, age 56 (1943)

A man knows when he is growing old
because he begins to look like his father.
Gabriel Garcia Marquez, age 57 (1985)

My mother protected me from the world
and my father threatened me with it.
Quentin Crisp, age 60 (1968)

In my culture, there is no such thing as a single woman alone with children. There is no such thing as "alone" at all. There is the family.

Miriam Makeba, age 55 (1987)

The thing that impresses me most about America is the way parents obey their children.

Edward, Duke of Windsor, age 63 (1957)

Our sons and daughters must be trained in national service, taught to give as well as to receive.

Emmeline Pankhurst, age 62 (1920)

Living en famille provides the strongest motives
for rudeness combined with the maximum
opportunity for displaying it.
Quentin Crisp, age 76 (1984)

As I sez, "Children and trees have to be tackled
young, Josiah, to bend their wills to the way
you want 'em to go."
Marietta Holley, age 63 (1899)

There would be no society if living together
depended upon understanding each other.
Eric Hoffer, age 71 (1973)

Keeping up with the Joneses was a full–time job
with my mother and father. It was not until
many years later when I lived alone that
I realized how much cheaper it was to
drag the Joneses down to my level.
Quentin Crisp, age 60 (1968)

POLITICS AND GOVERNMENT

If you're hanging around with nothing to do
and the zoo is closed, come over the Senate.
You'll get the same kind of feeling
and you won't have to pay.
Robert J. Dole, age 62 (1985)

No problem is more crucial than the achieving of a
world governing body capable of leading
a new type of harmonious world order...
Dorothy Gillam Baker, age 72 (1978)

All the ills of democracy can
be cured by more democracy.
Alfred E. Smith, age 60 (1933)

The contempt for law and the contempt for the human consequences of lawbreaking go from the bottom to the top of American society.
Margaret Mead, age 73 (1974)

If you're going to sin, sin against God, not the bureaucracy; God will forgive you but the bureaucracy won't.
Hyman G. Rickover, age 86 (1986)

My opponents can't get elected unless things get worse. And things aren't going to get worse unless they get elected.
George Bush, age 64 (1988)

Sure the people are stupid: the human race is stupid. Sure Congress is an inefficient instrument of government. But the people are not stupid enough to abandon representative government for any other kind, including government by the guy who knows.

Bernard Devoto, age 58 (1955)

A government big enough to give you everything you want is a government big enough to take from you everything you have.

Gerald R. Ford, age 63 (1976)

Two cheers for democracy: one because it admits
variety and two because it permits criticism.
E. M. Forster, age 72 (1951)

The first law of politics: Never say anything in a
national campaign that anyone might remember.
Eugene J. McCarthy, age 74 (1990)

One of the chief virtues of a democracy
is that its defects are always visible.
Harry S. Truman, age 63 (1947)

The secret of the Kennedy successes in politics was not money but meticulous planning and organization, tremendous effort and the enthusiasm and devotion of family and friends.
Rose Fitzgerald Kennedy, age 84 (1974)

If you tell Congress everything about the world situation, they get hysterical. If you tell them nothing, they go fishing.
Harry S. Truman, age 66 (1950)

If nominated, I will not accept.
If elected, I will not serve.
William Tecumseh Sherman, age 64 (1884)

If I am nominated [for the presidency], I will not
run. If I am elected, I will not serve. But if you
beg me, I just might reconsider.
Alexander M. Haig, age 63 (1987)

To make us love our country,
our country ought to be lovely.
Edmund Burke, age 61 (1790)

No influence so quickly converts a radical into a
reactionary as does his election to power.
Elisabeth Marbury, age 67 (1923)

Apparently, a democracy is a place where numerous elections are held at great cost without issues and with interchangeable candidates.

Gore Vidal, age 64 (1989)

The greatest enemy of individual freedom is the individual himself.

Saul Alinsky, age 62 (1971)

Patriotism is the last refuge of the scoundrel.

Samuel Johnson, age 66 (1775)

Too bad that all the people who know how to run the country are busy driving taxicabs and cutting hair.

George Burns, age 83 (1979)

Do not run a campaign that would embarrass your mother.

Robert C. Byrd, age 70 (1987)

The power to tax is the power to govern.

Maurice L. Duplessis, age 56 (1946)

If you purify the pond [referring to Congress], the water lilies die.

Eugene J. McCarthy age 74 (1990)

Freedom is not an ideal, it is not even a protection,
if it means nothing more than freedom to stagnate,
to live without dreams, to have no greater aim than
a second car and another television set.
Adlai Stevenson, age 60 (1960)

Like all the best families, we have our share
of eccentricities, of impetuous and wayward
youngsters and of family disagreements.
Queen Elizabeth II, age 63 (1989)

Governments last as long as the underrated
can defend them against the overtaxed.
Bernard Berenson, age 87 (1952)

Principles aren't of much account anyway,
except at election time. After that you hang
them up to let them season.
Mark Twain, age 66 (1901)

Collecting more taxes than is absolutely
necessary is legalized robbery.
Calvin Coolidge, age 83 (1955)

Finishing second in the Olympics gets you silver.
Finishing second in politics gets you oblivion.
Richard M. Nixon, age 75 (1988)

When the leaders choose to make themselves bidders at an auction of popularity, their talents, in the construction of the state, will be of no service. They will become flatterers instead of legislators; the instruments, not the guides, of the people.

Edmund Burke, age 61 (1790)

Patriots always talk of dying for their country and never of killing for their country.

Bertrand Russell, age 95 (1967)

The idea that you can merchandise candidates for high office like breakfast cereal—that you can gather votes like box tops—is, I think, the ultimate indignity to the democratic process.
Adlai Stevenson, age 56 (1956)

A politician will do anything to keep his job— even become a patriot.
William Randolph Hearst, age 68 (1933)

A government which robs Peter to pay Paul can always depend on the support of Paul.
George Bernard Shaw, age 88 (1944)

It could probably be shown by facts and figures that there is no distinctly native American criminal class except Congress.
Mark Twain, age 62 (1897)

In general, the art of government consists in taking as much money as possible from one party of the citizens to give to the other.
Voltaire, age 70 (1764)

A liberal is a conservative who has been arrested.
Tom Wolfe, age 56 (1987)

If you attack the establishment long enough and
hard enough, they will make you a member of it.
Art Buchwald, age 64 (1989)

Fleas can be taught nearly everything
that a Congressman can.
Mark Twain, age 71 (1906)

A good Congress is measured by laws that mean
something to people—p–e–e–p–u–l, p–e–e–p–l–e,
p–e–e–p–u–l—you know what I'm talkin' about,
just plain folks.
Lyndon B. Johnson, age 62 (1966)

There never was a good war or a bad peace.
Benjamin Franklin, age 77 (1783)

I would rather have peace in
the world than be President.
Harry S Truman, age 62 (1948)

Government does not solve problems;
it subsidizes them.
Ronald Reagan, age 61 (1972)

The essence of statesmanship is not a rigid
adherence to the past, but a prudent and
probing concern for the future.
Hubert H. Humphrey, age 56 (1967)

In statesmanship get the formalities right,
never mind about the moralities.
Mark Twain, age 62 (1897)

The law isn't justice. It's a very imperfect
mechanism. If you press exactly the right
buttons and are also lucky, justice may show
up in the answer. A mechanism is all the
law was ever intended to be.
Raymond Chandler, age 65 (1953)

Power tires only those who do not have it.
Giulio Andreotti, age 73 (1992)

We have had triumphs, we have
made mistakes, we have had sex.
George Bush, age 64 (1988) (regarding his
administration with President Reagan)

But there are advantages to being elected President.
The day after I was elected, I had my high
school grades classified Top Secret.
Ronald Reagan, age 75 (1986)

Power and violence are opposites; where the one
rules absolutely, the other is absent. Violence
appears where power is in jeopardy, but left to its
own course it ends in power's disappearance.
Hannah Arendt, age 66 (1972)

Courts of law, and all the paraphernalia and folly of
law … cannot be found in a rational state of society.
Robert Owen, age 62 (1833)

The real leader has no need to lead—
he is content to point the way.
Henry Miller, age 56 (1947)

As usual, the Liberals offer a mixture of sound
and original ideas. Unfortunately none of
the sound ideas is original and none of
the original ideas is sound.
Harold Macmillan, age 67 (1961)

The two–party system has given this country the war of Lyndon Johnson, the Watergate of Nixon, and the incompetence of Carter. Saying we should keep the two–party system simply because it is working is like saying the Titanic voyage was a success because a few people survived on life–rafts.

Eugene J. McCarthy, age 62 (1978)

Politicians are the same all over: they promise to build a bridge even where there is no river.

Nikita Khrushchev, age 66 (1960)

One has to be a lowbrow, a bit of a murderer,
to be a politician, ready and willing to see people
sacrificed, slaughtered, for the sake of an idea,
whether a good one or a bad one.

Henry Miller, age 72

Interview in Writers at Work (Second Series, ed. by
George Plimpton, 1963)

Nothing is so abject and pathetic as a politician
who has lost his job, save only a retired stud–horse.

H. L. Mencken, age 79 (1949)

Political image is like mixing cement.
When it's wet, you can move it around
and shape it, but at some point it hardens and
there's almost nothing you can do to reshape it.
Walter F. Mondale, age 63 (1991)

Practical politics consists in ignoring facts.
Henry B. Adams, age 69 (1907)

Politics is just like show business,
you have a hell of an opening, coast for
a while and then have a hell of a close.
Ronald Reagan, age 55 (1966)

RELIGION AND BELIEF

A belief is not true because it is useful.
Henri Frederic Amiel, age 55 (1876)

Religion is love; in no case is it logic.
Beatrice Potter Webb, age 68 (1926)

But men never violate the laws of God without
suffering the consequences, sooner or later.
Lydia M. Child, age 63 (1865)

To believe in something not yet proved and to
underwrite it with our lives: it is the only way we
can leave the future open. Man, surrounded by
facts, permitting himself no surmise,
no intuitive flash, no great hypothesis, no risk,
is in a locked cell. Ignorance cannot seal
the mind and imagination more surely.
Lillian Smith, age 57 (1954)

But a priest's life is not supposed to be well–
rounded; it is supposed to be one–pointed—
a compass, not a weathercock.
Aldous Huxley, age 58 (1952)

Euthanasia is a long, smooth–sounding word, and it
conceals its danger as long, smooth words do,
but the danger is there, nevertheless.
Pearl S. Buck, age 58 (1950)

None of us has lived up to the teachings of Christ.
Eleanor Roosevelt, age 62 (1946)

I think a bishop who doesn't give offence
to anyone is probably not a good bishop.
James Lawton Thompson, age 55 (1991)

Mind and spirit together make up that which
separates us from the rest of the animal world, that
which enables a man to know the truth and that
which enables him to die for the truth.
Edith Hamilton, age 63 (1930)

Absolute faith corrupts as
absolutely as absolute power.
Eric Hoffer, age 71 (1973)

We cannot always understand the ways of Almighty God—the crosses which He sends us, the sacrifices which He demands of us…But we accept with faith and resignation His holy will with no looking back to what might have been, and we are at peace.
Rose Fitzgerald Kennedy, age 78 (1968)

God never appears to you in person but always in action.
Mohandas Gandhi, age 59 (1928)

God should never have been expelled from America's classrooms in the first place.
Ronald Reagan, age 72 (1983)

SEX

Quite a few women told me, one way or another,
that they thought it was sex, not youth,
that's wasted on the young...
Janet Harris, age 60 (1975)

The sex symbol always remains, but the
sophisticated woman has become old hat.
Rosalind Russell, age 63 (1974)

The Englishman can get along with sex quite
perfectly so long as he can pretend that
it isn't sex but something else.
James Agate, age 55 (1932)

The best way to hold a man is in your arms.
Mae West, age 75 (1967)

Sex. In America an obsession.
In other parts of the world a fact.
Marlene Dietrich, age 69 (1962)

I find it extraordinary that a straightforward
if inelegant device for ensuring the survival
of the species should involve human beings
in such emotional turmoil. Does sex have
to be taken so seriously?
P. D. James, age 69 (1989)

I used to be Snow White...but I drifted.
Mae West, age 75 (1967)

There is nothing safe about sex. There never will be.
Norman Mailer, age 68 (1992)

SOCIAL ILLS

The children are always the
chief victims of social chaos.
Agnes Meyer, age 66 (1953)

I've never accepted any inferior role because
of my race or color. And by God, I never will.
Paul Robeson, age 61 (1949)

We [people of color] want to be accepted just as we
are, but at the same time we want the other person
to *win* the right to our acceptance of him.
Howard Thurman, age 63 (1963)

Nothing but ruin stares a nation in the
face that is a prey to the drink habit.
Mohandas Gandhi, age 60 (1929)

My grandmother, when she heard that Mr. Lincoln
had abolished slavery and the Negroes were free,
was heard to say "I hope it works both ways,"
and lived to realize that it did not.
Katherine Anne Porter, age 85 (1975)

We must do something and we must do it now. We
must educate the white people out of their
two hundred fifty years of slave history.
Ida B. Wells, age 66 (1928)

Napoleon was not different from the slum kid who tries to take over the block, he just had big armies through which to amplify his aggression.

Ralph Ellison, age 72 (1986)

I am above eighty years old; it is about time for me to be going. I have been forty years a slave and forty years free, and would be here forty years more to have equal rights for all. I suppose I am kept here because something remains for me to do; I suppose I am yet to help break the chain.

Sojourner Truth, age 70 (1867)

My mother could smell whiskey on your breath if
she was in the market and you were home in bed.
Eubie Blake, age 96 (1979)

Whatever the white man has done,
we have done, and often better.
Mary McLeod Bethune, age 63 (1938)

The heartless stupidity of those who have
never known a great and terrifying poverty.
Edith Sitwell, age 78 (1965)

SOCIETY

[Contemplating a party] Conversation did
not flow with the drink; it drowned in it.
Quentin Crisp, age 60 (1968)

I hold that gentleman to be the best–dressed
whose dress no one observes.
Anthony Trollope, age 64 (1879)

Wine gives a man nothing. It neither gives him knowledge nor wit; it only animates a man, and enables him to bring out what a dread of the company has repressed. It only puts in motion what had been locked up in frost.

Samuel Johnson, age 59

Quoted in: James Boswell's *Life of Samuel Johnson*, 28 April 1778 (1791)

True eloquence consists in saying all that need be said and no more.

François, Duc De La Rochefoucauld, age 65 (1678)

Nothing more rapidly inclines a person to go into
a monastery than reading a book on etiquette.
There are so many trivial ways in which it is
possible to commit some social sin.
Quentin Crisp, age 72 (1984)

Wine makes a man better pleased with himself.
I do not say that it makes him more pleasing to
others … This is one of the disadvantages of wine,
it makes a man mistake words for thoughts.
Samuel Johnson, age 59

Quoted in: James Boswell's *Life of Samuel Johnson*,
28 April 1778 (1791)

At every party there are two kinds of people—
those who want to go home and those
who don't. The trouble is, they are usually
married to each other.
Ann Landers, age 73 (1991)

THE SPOKEN WORD

One always tends to overpraise a long book,
because one has got through it.
E. M. Forster, age 56 (1935)

Slang is a language that rolls up its sleeves,
spits on its hands, and goes to work.
Carl Sandburg, age 81 (1959)

Speech is power: speech is to persuade, to convert,
to compel. It is to bring another out of his
bad sense into your good sense.
Ralph Waldo Emerson, age 73 (1876)

I do not object to people looking at their watches
when I am speaking. But I strongly object
when they start shaking them to make certain
they are still going.
Lord Birkett, age 77 (1960)

Give the people a new word and they
think they have a new fact.
Willa Cather, age 60 (1936)

Words are, of course, the most powerful
drug used by mankind.
Rudyard Kipling, age 58 (1923)

One forgets words as one forgets names.
One's vocabulary needs constant fertilizing
or it will die.
Evelyn Waugh, age 59 (1962)

SUCCESS AND FAILURE

If there is a faith that can move mountains,
it is faith in your own power.
Marie Ebner von Eschenbach, age 75 (1905)

If initiative is the ability to do the right thing,
then efficiency is the ability to do the thing right.
Kelly Miller, age 81 (1944)

Nothing is more difficult than
competing with a myth.
Francoise Giroud, age 58 (1974)

You have the ability, now apply yourself.
Benjamin Mays, age 76 (1971)

Behind every man who achieves success
Stand a mother, a wife, and the IRS.
Ethel Jacobson, age 68 (1973)

God gives every bird his worm,
but He does not throw it into the nest.
P. D. James, age 69 (1989)

Always strive to excel, but only on weekends.
Richard Rorty, age 58 (1990)

I can honestly say that I was never affected by
the question of the success of an undertaking.
If I felt it was the right thing to do, I was for
it regardless of the possible outcome.
Golda Meir, age 66 (1964)

What we call luck is the inner man externalized.
We make things happen to us.
Robertson Davies, age 72 (1985)

Chance is the one thing you can't buy ... You have
to pay for it and you have to pay for it with your
life, spending a lot of time, you pay for it with time,
not the wasting of time but the spending of time.
Robert Doisneau, age 80 (1992)

He loved his dreams and cultivated them.
Colette, age 60 (1933)

The man with a new idea is a
crank until the idea succeeds.
Mark Twain, age 62 (1897)

This shall be my parting word—know what you
want to do—then do it. Make straight for your
goal and go undefeated in spirit to the end.
Ernestine Schumann–Heink, age 74 (1935)

The test of a vocation is the love
of the drudgery it involves.
Logan Pearsall Smith, age 66 (1931)

The best is the enemy of the good.
Voltaire, age 70 (1764)

We should be careful to get out of an experience only the wisdom that is in it—and stop there; lest we be like the cat that sits down on a hot stove–lid. She will never sit down on a hot stove–lid again—and that is well; but also she will never sit down on a cold one anymore.
Mark Twain, age 62 (1897)

Trying to be fascinating is an asinine position to be in.
Katherine Hepburn, age 66 (1975)

We are all failures—at least, all the best of us are.
J. M. Barrie, age 62 (1922)

Every man is born into the world to do something
unique and something distinctive and if he or she
does not do it, it will never be done.
Benjamin E. Mays, age 86 (1981)

Ever tried. Ever failed. No matter.
Try Again. Fail again. Fail better.
Samuel Beckett, age 78 (1984)

I cannot give you the formula for success,
but I can give you the formula for failure—
which is: Try to please everybody.
Herbert B. Swope, age 68 (1950)

A legend is an old man with a cane known
for what he used to do. I'm still doing it.
Miles Davis, age 65 (1991)

A celebrity is one who is known to many
persons he is glad he doesn't know.
H. L. Mencken, age 69 (1949)

The toughest thing about success is that you've got
to keep on being a success. Talent is only a starting
point in this business. You've got to keep
on working that talent. Someday I'll
reach for it and it won't be there.
Irving Berlin, age 70 (1958)

Always aim high, never aim low. If you aspire to
lofty things, you have accomplished much even
though you have not reached the topmost round.
William Hastie, age 80 (1984)

There is a vast difference between success at twenty–five and success at sixty. At sixty, nobody envies you. Instead, everybody rejoices generously, sincerely, in your good fortune.

Marie Dressler, age 61 (1934)

God doesn't require us to succeed;
he only requires that you try.

Mother Teresa, age 82 (New York, Dec. 1992)

It takes little talent to see clearly what lies under one's nose, a good deal of it to know in which direction to point that organ.

W. H. Auden, age 55 (1962)

If a man can write a better book, preach a better sermon, or make a better mouse–trap, than his neighbor, though he build his house in the woods, the world will make a beaten path to his door.

Ralph Waldo Emerson, age 68 (1871)

It is better to be a has–been than a never–was.

Cecil Parkinson, age 58 (1990)

Mediocrity knows nothing higher than itself, but talent instantly recognizes genius.

Sir Arthur Conan Doyle, age 56 (1915)

To get it right, be born with luck or else make it. Never give up. Get the knack of getting people to help you and also pitch in yourself. A little money helps, but what really gets it right is to never—I repeat—never under any conditions face the facts.

Ruth Gordon, age 74 (1970)

What makes us so bitter against people who outwit us is that they think themselves cleverer than we are.

François, Duc De La Rochefoucauld, age 65 (1678)

It is not real work unless you would rather be doing something else.

J. M. Barrie, age 62 (1922)

It's true hard work never killed anybody,
but I figure, why take the chance?
Ronald Reagan, age 76 (1987)

TELEVISION

Television's perfect. You turn a few knobs, a few of those mechanical adjustments at which the higher apes are so proficient, and lean back and drain your mind of all thought. And there you are watching the bubbles in the primeval ooze. You don't have to concentrate. You don't have to react. You don't have to remember. You don't miss your brain because you don't need it. Your heart and liver and lungs continue to function normally. Apart from that, all is peace and quiet. You are in the man's nirvana. And if some poor nasty minded person comes along and says you look like a fly on a can of garbage, pay him no mind. He probably hasn't got the price of a television set.

Raymond Chandler, age 62 (1950)

Television thrives on unreason, and unreason thrives on television. It strikes at the emotions rather than the intellect.
Sir Robin Day, age 74 (1989)

It is a medium of entertainment which permits millions of people to listen to the same joke at the same time, and yet remain lonesome.
T. S. Eliot, age 75 (1963)

Television, despite its enormous presence, turns out to have added pitifully few lines to the communal memory.
Justin Kaplan, age 66 (1991)

I find television very educational.
Every time someone switches it on I go
into another room and read a good book.
Groucho Marx, age (unknown)

Quoted in: Leslie Halliwell, *Halliwell's Filmgoer's
Companion* (1984)

Television brought the brutality of war into the
comfort of the living room. Vietnam was lost in
the living rooms of America—not on the
battlefields of Vietnam.
Marshall McLuhan, age 64 (1975)

In Westerns you were permitted to
kiss your horse but never your girl.
Gary Cooper, age 57 (1958)

TOURISM AND TRAVEL

The American arrives in Paris with a few French
phrases he has culled from a conversational guide or
picked up from a friend who owns a beret.
Fred Allen, age 60 (1954)

In the middle ages people were tourists because of
their religion, whereas now they are tourists
because tourism is their religion.
Robert Runcie, age 67 (1988)

When one realizes that his life is worthless
he either commits suicide or travels.
Edward Dahlberg, age 65 (1965)

A journey is like marriage. The certain way
to be wrong is to think you control it.
John Steinbeck, age 59 (1961)

WAR AND PEACE

When war is declared, truth is the first casualty.
Arthur Ponsonby, age 57 (1928)

All war represents a failure of diplomacy.
Tony Benn, age 55 (1991)

A leader who doesn't hesitate before he sends
his nation into battle is not fit to be a leader.
Golda Meir, age 69 (1967)

Morality is contraband in war.
Mohandas K. Gandhi, age 73 (1942)

For it isn't enough to talk about peace.
One must believe in it. And it isn't enough
to believe in it. One must work at it.
Eleanor Roosevelt, age 67 (1951)

The most persistent sound which reverberates
through man's history is the beating of war drums.
Arthur Koestler, age 72 (1978)

The more prosperous and settled a nation, the
more readily it tends to think of war as a regrettable
accident; to nations less fortunate the chance of war
presents itself as a possible bountiful friend.
Lewis H. Lapham, age 56 (1991)

We are not interested in the possibilities of defeat.
Queen Victoria, age 80 (1899)

You cannot shake hands with a clenched fist.
Indira Gandhi, age 55 (1972)

More than an end to war, we want
an end to the beginnings of all wars.
Franklin D. Roosevelt, age 62
(1945, written but never delivered)

I cannot believe that war is the best solution.
No one won the last war, and no one will
win the next one.
Eleanor Roosevelt, age 63 (1948)

It is far easier to make war than to make peace.

Georges Clemenceau, age 70 (1919)

WIT AND WISDOM

The biggest sin is sitting on your ass.
Florynce R. Kennedy, Esq., age 57 (1973)

If only her brain worked as well as her jaws!
Colette, age 71 (1944)

Well, time wounds all heels.
Jane Ace, age 61 (1966)

Such is the nature of men, that howsoever they may acknowledge many others to be more witty, or more eloquent, or more learned; yet they will hardly believe there be many so wise as themselves.
Thomas Hobbes, age 63 (1651)

Fortunate are people whose roots are deep.
Agnes Meyer, age 66 (1953)

History teaches us that men and nations
behave wisely once they have exhausted
all other alternatives.
Abba Eban, age 55 (1970)

Dogs' lives are too short. Their only fault, really.
Carlotta Monteey O'Neill, age 84 (1972)

It is the province of knowledge to speak,
and it is the privilege of wisdom to listen.
Oliver Wendell Holmes, Sr., age 63 (1872)

The worst in life, we are told, is compatible with
the best in art. So too the worst in life is
compatible with the best in humour.
Agnes Repplier, age 78 (1936)

Experience shows that exceptions are as true as rules.
Edith Ronald Mirrielees, age 63 (1947)

Whoever is careless with the truth in small matters
cannot be trusted with important matters.
Albert Einstein, age 75 (1954)

If you keep things long enough, some fool
or other will come along an' buy 'em.
Carlotta Montee O'Neill, age 84 (1972)

Nine–tenths of wisdom consists
in being wise in time.
Theodore Roosevelt, age 59 (1917)

Silence is sweeter than speech.
Dinah Mulock Craik, age 61 (1887)

Wit is so shining a quality that everybody admires
it; most people aim at it, all people fear it,
and few love it unless in themselves. A man
must have a good share of wit himself to
endure a great share of it in another.
Lord Chesterfield, age 69 (1765)

There's a helluva distance between wisecracking
and wit. Wit has truth in it; wisecracking
is simply calisthenics with words.
Dorothy Parker, age 65 (1958)

Well, I've gotten to the end of the subject—end of
the page—of your patience and my time.
Alice B. Toklas, age 72 (1949)

In nature nothing creates itself
and nothing destroys itself.
Maria Montessori, age 69 (1939)

Then all will be over,
bar the shouting and the worms.
Edith Sitwell, age 78 (1965)

She quoted a friend who used to say any advice
is good as long as it is strong enough.
Alice B. Toklas, age 69 (1946)

The wisdom of silence is a great asset.
De Alva Stanwood Alexander, age 70 (1916)

THE WRITTEN "PRINTED" WORD

Sometimes…it takes me an entire day to
write a recipe, to communicate it correctly.
It's really like writing a little short story…
Julia Child, age 58 (1970)

Writing a novel is not merely going on a shopping
expedition across the border to an unreal land:
it is hours and years spent in the factories,
the streets, the cathedrals of the imagination.
Janet Frame, age 61 (1985)

The more the data banks record about
each one of us, the less we exist.
Marshall McLuhan, age 58 (1969)

Frankly, despite my horror of the press,
I'd love to rise from the grave every ten
years or so and go buy a few newspapers.
Luis Buñuel, age 83 (1983)

Newspapers are unable, seemingly,
to discriminate between a bicycle accident
and the collapse of civilisation.
George Bernard Shaw, age 75 (1931)

The world may be full of fourth–rate writers
but it's also full of fourth–rate readers.
Stan Barstow, age 61 (1989)

A classic—something that everybody wants
to have read and nobody wants to read.
Mark Twain, age 65 (1900)

The unread story is not a story; it is little black
marks on wood pulp. The reader, reading it,
makes it live: a live thing, a story.
Ursula K. Le Guin, age 60 (1989)

With one day's reading a man
may have the key in his hands.
Ezra Pound, age 63 (1948)

A best–seller is the gilded tomb of a mediocre talent.
Logan Pearsall Smith, age 66 (1931)

There are books … which take rank in your life
with parents and lovers and passionate experiences,
so medicinal, so stringent, so revolutionary,
so authoritative.
Ralph Waldo Emerson, age 67 (1870)

Power without responsibility—the prerogative of
the harlot throughout the ages.
[Speaking of the press]
Stanley Baldwin, age 64 (1931)

No poet or novelist wishes he were the only one
who ever lived, but most of them wish they were
the only one alive, and quite a number fondly
believe their wish has been granted.

W. H. Auden, age 56 (1963)

An author who speaks about his own books
is almost as bad as a mother who talks about
her own children.

Benjamin Disraeli, age 69 (1873)

If I had not existed, someone else would have
written me, Hemingway, Dostoevski, all of us.

William Faulkner, age 61 (1958)

The shelf life of the modern hardback writer is
somewhere between the milk and the yogurt.
John Mortimer, age 64 (1987)

I cringe when critics say I'm a master of the
popular novel. What's an unpopular novel?
Irwin Shaw, age 70 (1983)

Writing is a socially acceptable
form of schizophrenia.
E. L. Doctorow, age 57 (1988)

Habits in writing as in life are only useful if they are
broken as soon as they cease to be advantageous.
W. Somerset Maugham, age 64 (1938)

It's hard enough to write a good drama,
it's much harder to write a good comedy,
and it's hardest of all to write a drama
with comedy. Which is what life is.
Jack Lemmon, age 65 (1990)

Buying books would be a good thing if one
could also buy the time to read them in:
but as a rule the purchase of books is mistaken
for the appropriation of their contents.
Arthur Schopenhauer, age 63 (1851)

That is a good book which is opened with
expectation and closed with profit.
A. Bronson Alcott, age 78 (1877)